Flute / Oboe / Mallet Percussion

Easy Great Carols

Instrumental Solos for the Intermediate Soloist

Contents

CURNOW MUSIC

EXCLUSIVELY DISTRIBUTED BY

HAL•LEONARD CORPORATION

7777 W. BLUEMOUND RD. P.O. BOX 13819 MILWAUKEE, WI 53213

Selected by James Curnow

Easy Great Carols
Flute / Oboe / Mallet Percussion

Arranged by:
Stephen Bulla
Douglas Court
James Curnow
Paul Curnow
Timothy Johnson

Order number: CMP 0920.04
ISBN 978-90-431-2028-9
CD number: 19.052-3 CMP

Easy Great Carols

INTRODUCTION

These carols, collected from around the world, include both sacred and whimsical selections. The arrangements have been created by some of the foremost writers of instrumental music, who are internationally known for their musical compositions and arrangements. The goal of these arrangements is to allow the instrumentalist the opportunity to give praise and adoration to God through their musical abilities.

There is a separate piano accompaniment book available. This accompaniment book will work with all of the soloist books. When an accompanist is not available, the accompaniment CD (included) can be used for performance. This CD will also allow the soloist to rehearse on their own when an accompanist is not available.

The accompaniment CD contains tuning notes at the beginning to allow the soloist to adjust their intonation to the intonation of the compact disc accompaniment. Each arrangement in this collection includes a sample performance with soloist as well as a track with just the accompaniment.

May you enjoy using this collection and find it useful in extending your musical ministry.

Kindest regards,

James Curnow
President
Curnow Music Press

1. HARK! THE HERALD ANGELS SING

Track: 3 13

Arr. **James Curnow** (ASCAP)

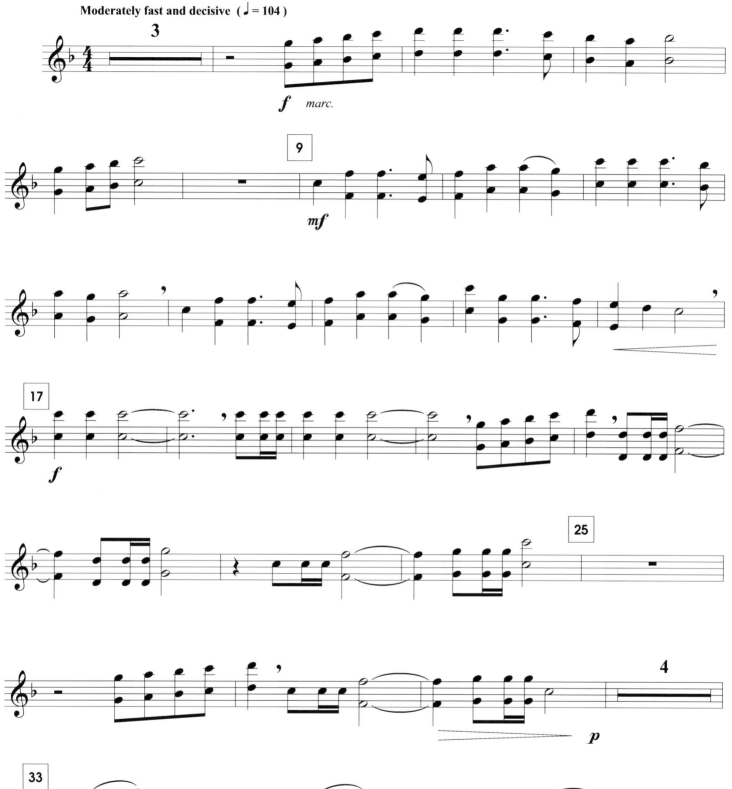

Copyright © 2004 by **Curnow Music Press, Inc.**

2. SILENT NIGHT

Arr. **Paul Curnow** (ASCAP)

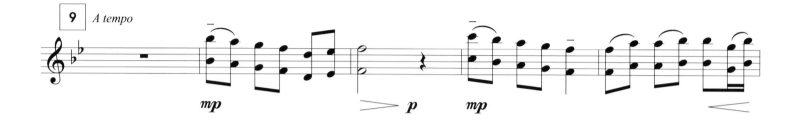

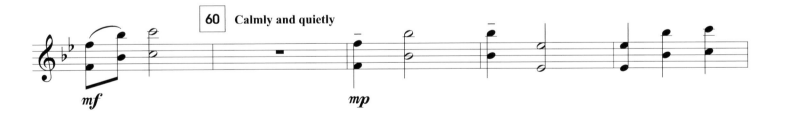

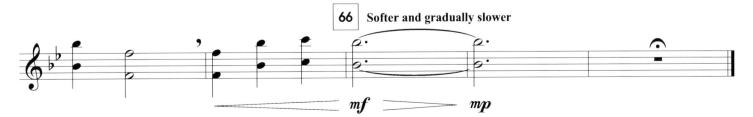

3. WE THREE KINGS

Arr. **Timothy Johnson** (ASCAP)

Copyright © 2004 by **Curnow Music Press, Inc.**

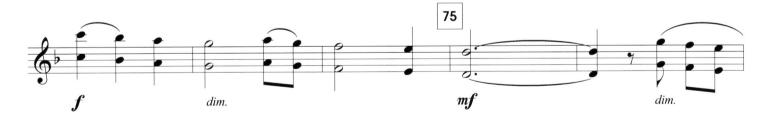

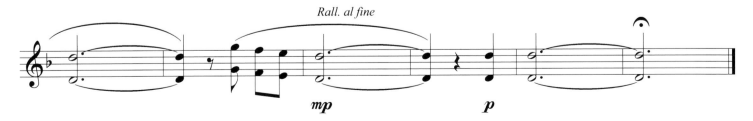

4. GOD REST YE MERRY, GENTLEMEN

Track: **6 16**

Arr. **Stephen Bulla** (ASCAP)

Moderately fast (♩ = 84)

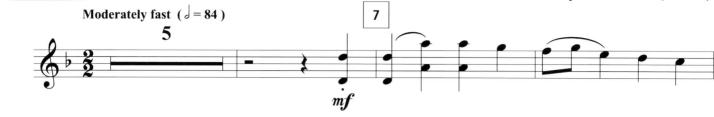

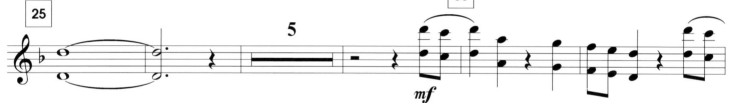

5. JOLLY OLD ST. NICHOLAS

Track: 7 17

Arr. **Douglas Court** (ASCAP)

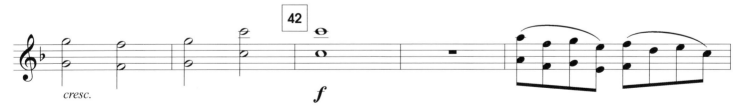

CMP 0920.04 Flute / Oboe / Mallet Percussion

6. PAT-A-PAN

Arr. **Stephen Bulla** (ASCAP)

7. AWAY IN A MANGER

Arr. **James Curnow** (ASCAP)

Track: 9 19

CMP 0920.04 Flute / Oboe / Mallet Percussion

Copyright © 2004 by **Curnow Music Press, Inc.**

13

8. UP ON THE HOUSETOP

Theme and Mini Variations

Arr. **Paul Curnow** (ASCAP)

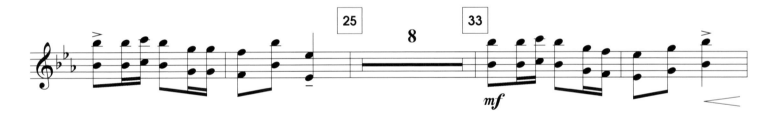

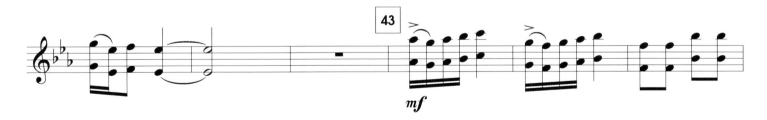

9. WE WISH YOU A MERRY CHRISTMAS

Arr. **Douglas Court** (ASCAP)

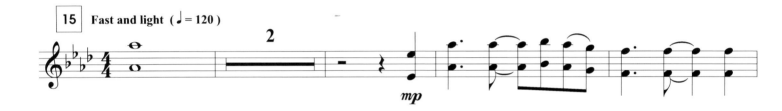

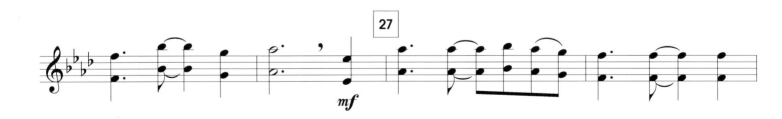

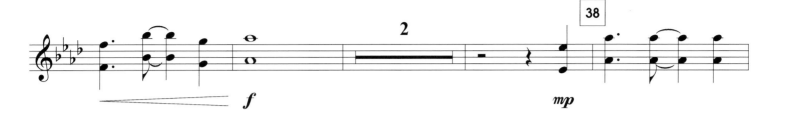

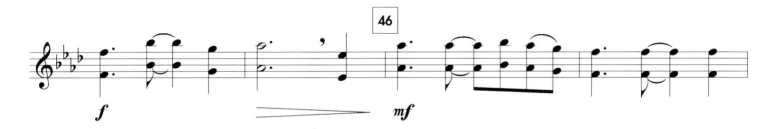

10. COVENTRY CAROL

Track: 12/22

Arr. **Timothy Johnson** (ASCAP)

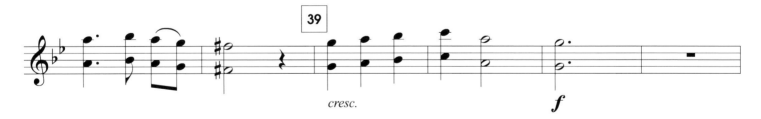